Rock Climbing

The World's Hottest Climbing Locations and Techniques

by Paul Mason

CAPSTONE PRESS

a capstone imprint

Edge Books are published by
Capstone Press, a Capstone imprint,
151 Good Counsel Drive, P.O. Box 669,
Mankato, Minnesota 56002.
www.capstonepub.com

First published 2011
Copyright © 2011 A & C Black
Publishers Limited

Produced for A & C Black by
Monkey Puzzle Media Ltd,
48 York Avenue,
Hove BN3 1PJ, UK

032010
005746ACF10

The right of Paul Mason to be identified as the
author of this Work has been asserted by him
in accordance with the Copyright, Designs, and
Patents Act 1988.

Library of Congress Cataloging-in-Publication
Data
Mason, Paul, 1967-
  Rock climbing: The World's Hottest Climbing
Locations and Techniques / by Paul Mason.
  p. cm. -- (Passport to World Sports)
  Includes index.
  ISBN 978-1-4296-5500-2 (library binding)
1. Rock climbing--Juvenile literature. I. Title.
II. Series.

GV200.2.M36 2011
796.52'2--dc22

2010008900

Editor: Dan Rogers
Design: Mayer Media Ltd
Picture research: Lynda Lines

This book is produced using paper that
is made from wood grown in managed,
sustainable forests. It is natural, renewable,
and recyclable. The logging and manufacturing
processes conform to the environmental
regulations of the country of origin.

Picture acknowledgements
Action Images pp. 6 (Sporting Pictures), 14–15
(Xavier Cailhol/DPPI Speed), 22 (Reuters/Yuriko
Nakao), 23 (Reuters/Yuriko Nakao); Zoltan
Bereczki p. 20; Corbis pp. 15 top (Karma/
Xinhua Press), 21 (Olivier Cadeaux), 25 Jon
Sparks; EICA p. 10; Getty Images pp. 1 (James
Balog), 8 (Josh McCulloch), 16 (Travel Ink), 24
(James Balog), 26–27 (Corey Rich), 28 (Kevin
Steele), 29 (Kevin Steele); iStockphoto pp.
7, 18; Paul Mason pp. 5, 9, 11, 13, 17, 19;
Photolibrary pp. 4 (Michael Meisl), 12 (Aurora
Photos). Compass rose artwork on front cover
and inside pages by iStockphoto. Map artwork
by MPM Images.

The front cover shows a female climber on a
rock face in the Dolomites mountains, Italy
(Photolibrary/Michael Meisl).

Every effort has been made to contact copyright
holders of material reproduced in this book.
Any omissions will be rectified in subsequent
printings if notice is given to the publishers.

SAFETY ADVICE

Rock climbing can be
extremely dangerous. Don't
attempt any of the activities
or techniques in this book
without the guidance of a
qualified instructor.

CONTENTS

It's a Rocky World

You're 33 feet (10 meters) up a rock face, almost at the safety of the ledge—but your arms are getting tired! Just in time, you spot a little crack. Jam your fingers in, move your leg higher, and pull upward. Made it! Now you can sit down comfortably, get your breath back, and enjoy the view. It's all part of the thrill of rock climbing.

ROCK CLIMBING WORLD

At any moment in time, the sun is shining on a rock-climbing route somewhere. But if you had a dream ticket that would take you anywhere in the world, which rock-climbing locations would you visit? And if you turned up there, would you fit in OK? Would you know the difference between a **chickenhead** and a **sloper**, for example?

Not an ideal route for beginners! Fortunately, there will be easier climbs nearby.

THE SECRET LANGUAGE OF CLIMBING

chickenhead bulging lump of rock (and also the name of a handhold)
sloper sloping (and not very good) handhold
harness safety equipment fastening around the waist and thighs

The climber on the left is about to set out. Both climbers are wearing safety harnesses.

PASSPORT TO THE WORLD OF ROCK

This book is your passport to the world of rock climbing. We'll tell you everything you need to know to fit right in with the other climbers:

• discover the secret language of climbing

• get advice on equipment, techniques, and other essentials

• visit some of the world's most amazing climbing sites—from routes where climbers can fall off into warm water to climbs that take days to finish.

Technical: Climbing kit

Most people start climbing on a course or with experienced friends. Once they get the climbing bug, though, they often end up buying their own equipment.

Climbing gear:

• Loose or stretchy tops and bottoms, so that you can move freely.

• Special rock-climbing shoes with sticky-rubber soles.

• Warm top to wear while waiting for someone else to climb.

Safety gear:

• Climbing rope and carabiners, for stopping climbers from falling.

• A **harness**, which attaches to the rope and holds you safely if you slip or fall.

• Helmet, in case of falls or rocks coming down from above.

Other equipment:

• Chalk bag (contains chalk for drying your fingertips while climbing).

• Figure-8 or other belay device for gripping the rope tightly.

• Tool for removing equipment from cracks in the rock.

Chamonix Valley

Where better to start climbing than on some of the world's first-ever routes? The Chamonix Valley contains some of the oldest climbing routes in the world. It's one of the places where the sport of rock climbing first developed.

WHY CHAMONIX?

Chamonix has something for everyone, not only for beginners. There are plenty of easy rock faces to practice on safely, of course. But some of the world's best climbers spend the summer here. On days when you aren't climbing yourself, you can watch the experts and try to pick up some tips.

"Topping out" (finishing) a route up one of the famous aiguilles, or needles, near Chamonix.

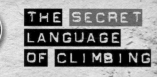

CHAMONIX VALLEY
Location: Haute Savoie, France
Type of climbing: all types
Difficulty level: between 1 and 5 of 5
Best season: June to September

THE SECRET LANGUAGE OF CLIMBING

topping out reaching the top of a climb

bouldering climbing at a low level, not usually higher than 6.5 feet (2 meters), with just a crash mat for safety gear

Tip from a Local
If you don't want to climb
using a rope, check out the
bouldering at Col des Montets.

WHERE TO CLIMB

Beginners: Beginners will find
great climbing around the lake
at Gaillands. This is also a good
spot for a picnic.

Intermediate climbers: The long,
open rock face at Vallorcine has
several routes for intermediate
climbers—plus amazing views
toward Switzerland!

Experts: Servoz offers plenty
of chances to practice climbing
past overhangs.

Other tips: If it's raining, the indoor
climbing wall at Les Houches is one
of the biggest in France.

*This young woman is on a sport-climbing
route—a tricky-looking one.*

Information: Types of climb

There are four main types of climbing. Some are suitable for all climbers;
others (such as soloing) are definitely experts only!

Top-roped climbing	Sport climbing	Traditional climbing	Soloing
Suitable for all climbers. The rope is fixed to a point above you, making a fall impossible.	For intermediates and experts. The rope attaches to fixed points on the rock, making long falls unlikely.	For intermediates and experts. The rope is temporarily attached to the rock, and if it comes loose, long falls are possible.	Even many experts dislike soloing, which is climbing alone.

Whistler

There's something to suit every climber on the rocks around Whistler. There are plenty of easy, short routes to practice on. Or you can spend the day watching climbers heading up the giant cliffs of the famous Stawamus Chief, the second-largest **granite** rock face in the world. Just make sure you bring binoculars—they'll be a long way away!

WHISTLER
Location: British Columbia, Canada
Type of climbing: all types
Difficulty level: between 1 and 5 of 5
Best season: June to September

WHY WHISTLER?

Every kind of climb can be found here, from routes that need careful balance to ones that demand lots of strength. The rock faces around Whistler are of tough, grippy granite. Your shoes and fingertips will stick to the rock face well. Sometimes too well—you might end up leaving a bit of skin behind on one of the handholds!

A long way above the ground, and a long reach to a handhold—climbing at Cheakamus Canyon, Whistler.

THE SECRET LANGUAGE OF CLIMBING

granite hard rock with surface like sandpaper

Harness safety

WHERE TO CLIMB

Beginners: The Squamish area has some of the best short routes in the area, and there is plenty here for beginners to do.

Intermediate climbers: Showcase Spire, a steep needle of rock on Blackcomb Mountain, would be a real challenge to do with a more experienced climber as a guide.

Tying a rope to your harness is a basic climbing skill. Learning to do this properly means you will always be safely attached to the rope—very important!

Put a loop into the end of the rope, with about 6.5 feet (2 meters) loose at the end.

Pass the end under the rope, then down through the loop, to make a figure 8.

Tip from a Local

If you want a day off from climbing, try the local mountain-bike trails—they're some of the best in the world!

Pass the end through your harness loop or carabiner.

Feed it back through the figure 8.

If you like Whistler ...

you could also try:
• Glencoe, Scotland
• Yosemite Valley, California
Both offer a real big-mountain experience.

Pull the whole knot tight.

Edinburgh International Climbing Arena

In the 1970s and 1980s, climbers started training indoors when the weather was bad. They nailed **holds** to the walls and ceilings of basements or garages, and clambered about to build strength. Since then, indoor climbing has come a long way. One of the world's best indoor walls is the Edinburgh International Climbing Arena.

EDINBURGH
Location: Edinburgh, Scotland
Type of climbing: top-roped, sport, bouldering
Difficulty level: between 1 and 5 of 5
Best season: all year

The Edinburgh Arena, with a bouldering area in the center, surrounded by crash mats.

THE SECRET LANGUAGE OF CLIMBING

holds places where your hands and/or feet can grip the rock

crash mat thickly padded safety mat

anchor point secure place to attach a climbing rope

WHY THE EDINBURGH ARENA?

The Arena is an amazing sight: this is one of the largest indoor climbing walls in the world. It's no accident that it's in Scotland—the weather outside is often cold and wet! In here, though, you're dry and warm, and there's a choice of almost every kind of climb to try.

Tip from a Local

Try Aerial Assault at the Edinburgh Arena—it's a bit like a normal assault course, but 100 feet (30 meters) above the ground!

Climbing at the Arena

The Arena offers climbing of most kinds, at every possible grade. The two best for beginners are the top-roping and bouldering areas:

Top-roping: The Arena's top-roped routes, which can be over 33 feet (10 meters) high, offer beginners climbing in complete safety.

Bouldering: The Bouldering Cavern is filled with tricky technical problems, which will have you crashing safely onto the **crash mats** time after time!

If you like Edinburgh ...

you could also try:
• Les Houches climbing wall, France
• Extreme Edge climbing wall, New Zealand
• Stoneworks climbing wall, Texas

A typical belay device: this kind is called a figure 8.

Top-roped climbing

Almost all climbers first experience climbing through top-roped climbs. This is a safe but exciting way to get into the sport.

A top-roped climb, with the climber almost at the top and the belayer watching carefully.

1. In top-roped climbing, the rope stretches up above the climber, through a secure **anchor point**, and back to the ground.

2. The climber's helper, called the belayer, grips the rope tightly in a belay device. He or she pulls it in as the climber moves up the route.

3. If the climber slips or falls, the rope stops him or her from dropping to the ground. It's still scary, of course!

4. Once the climber reaches the top, the belayer gently lowers him or her back down to the ground.

11

Las Conchas

The state of New Mexico is a rock climber's playground. For most of the year it offers warm-weather climbing on an amazing variety of rock. Whatever kind of climbing you're after, New Mexico has it all, from low-level bouldering to 985-foot (300-meter) climbs. Fortunately, there are plenty of wonderful places for beginners to learn.

LAS CONCHAS
Location: New Mexico
Type of climbing: top-roped
Difficulty level: 2.5 of 5
Best season: May to October

WHY LAS CONCHAS?

The climbs at Las Conchas are mainly between 33 and 66 feet (10 and 20 meters) high. They are usually climbed using a top-rope, which makes them very safe for beginners once the rope is set up properly. The technical difficulty of some routes is high, so this is an ideal place to test yourself without worrying about the dangers of a fall!

New Mexico has climbing to suit almost every ability level, and just about every type of climbing, too. This is Lisa Noel, climbing near Socorro.

THE SECRET LANGUAGE OF CLIMBING

crab short for carabiner, a loop of metal with a lockable gate in it

sling loop of strong nylon tape or rope

CLIMBING IN NORTHERN NEW MEXICO

Beginners: Las Conchas is ideal for beginners because of the short routes and top ropes, but Cochiti Mesa Crags also have easier routes. Climbers need a 4x4 vehicle to get to them, though!

Intermediate climbers: White Rock Canyon has plenty of harder routes for improving climbers to test themselves on. This is a busy area, so there will be lots of opportunities to get tips from other climbers.

Tip from a Local

New Mexico can be very hot, especially in summer—don't forget your sunscreen and water.

If you like Las Conchas ...

you could also try:
• Harrison's Rocks, England
• Gorge du Verdon, France (where some people say top-roping was invented)
Both have great top-roped routes.

TECHNIQUE
Fixing an anchor

When top-roping, it is crucial for the rope to be anchored securely at the top of the climb:

1. Check that the anchor point is solid and use a **crab** to attach a **sling** to the anchor. Screw the crab shut, then undo it half a turn. This stops it from getting jammed closed when the rope has weight on it.

2. Attach a second crab to the other end of the sling, and check that the crab dangles just over the edge of the climb. (This is important so that when the rope goes through the crab, it does not rub.) This should give a safe anchor point for the rope. You can now put the middle of the rope into the second crab.

When the rope is attached, throw it out and down so that both ends reach the bottom of the climb. (Always shout "BELOW!" when you do this, as a warning).

Climbing World Cup: Speed

Climbing is a tricky sport at the best of times. Imagine how much harder it would be if you had to do everything quickly! But that's just what happens in speed climbing competitions. On the plus side, watching one of these contests, rather than taking part in one, is very thrilling.

THE IFSC AND THE WORLD CUP

The International Federation of Sport Climbing (IFSC) is the governing body for climbing contests around the world. Its top-level competition is the World Cup. This is a series of events around the world, where top climbers gather to see who can climb best. Once all the events are finished, whoever has won the most points during the year is the winner.

SPEED-CLIMBING WALLS

If you want to set a world record for speed climbing, you have to climb on an officially recognized wall. These are either 33 or 49 feet (10 or 15 meters) high. They have a 5 degree **overhang**, and each wall has exactly the same sequence of handholds and footholds. So whether you are climbing at the Shou Shan Middle School in Taiwan, or the Rock Master Stadium in Arco di Trento, Italy, the moves you need to get to the top don't change.

Speed Records

In 2009, two new world records were set for 49-foot (15-meter) speed climbing. Qixin Zhong set the men's record at 6.64 seconds. He Cuilian set the women's record at 9.04 seconds.

Speed climbing is fairly simple—fastest to the top wins. These climbers are at the 2008 European championships.

Tip from an Expert
In the late 1990s, Dan Osman climbed the 400-foot (122-meter) Lover's Leap in California. He did it without ropes in an astonishing time of 4 minutes and 25 seconds.

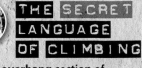

THE SECRET LANGUAGE OF CLIMBING

overhang section of rock face that slopes outward

The start of a men's heat at the speed-climbing world championships in Xining, China, in 2009.

Technical: How speed climbing contests work

Speed climbing is one of the most exciting climbing contest formats. What should you expect if you go to see one of these events?

1. Contests usually follow a sudden-death knockout format. All the climbers take part in qualification, with the eight fastest making it into the quarterfinals.

2. After this, pairs of climbers race each other up identical side-by-side routes. The first to the top goes through to the semifinals round. The loser leaves the competition.

3. The four semifinalists race for places in the final, after which one more climb decides the winner.

15

Stanage Edge

The dramatic scenery of Stanage Edge is probably the most famous climbing area in England. The line of **gritstone** cliffs stretch for 4.3 miles (7 kilometers). The grippy rock makes this a great location for improving your **friction climbing**.

WHY STANAGE EDGE?

There are well over 1,000 different climbs at Stanage. They include some of the world's very first rock routes, and these are ideal for a first taste of climbing at Stanage. The heartland of British climbing, the city of Sheffield, is nearby, so there are also plenty of more challenging climbs for intermediate climbers and experts.

STANAGE EDGE
Location: Derbyshire, England
Type of climbing: top-roped, bouldering, traditional
Difficulty level: 1 to 4.5 of 5
Best season: May to September

CLIMBING AT STANAGE EDGE

Beginners and intermediate climbers: There are good routes for beginners and intermediate climbers all along Stanage Edge. Most easy routes follow the lines of cracks in the rock face. Just pick a crack, fix a top rope, and give it a try.

Experts: The route of Archangel at Goliath's Groove tests even the bravest climber. Next door is Ulysses, which only the most expert climbers can hope to get up.

Stanage Edge is one of the oldest climbing locations in England. Some climbs were first done by Victorians wearing tweed suits and hobnailed boots.

Friction holds

If you like Stanage ...

you'd better just go back to Stanage. There isn't really anywhere else quite like it.

On most climbs, there are two types of holds. One is a nice, solid-feeling space where you can put your fingers or toes for grip. The other is a friction hold. Friction holds are especially effective for your feet, which are equipped with sticky-soled climbing shoes:

Smearing the toe of your shoe against the rock and letting your weight sink onto it will give you a good, balanced position on the rock face.

Tip from a Local

Take a warm jacket— Stanage is high up and open to the wind, so it can be chilly.

Sometimes you have to use the inside edge of your foot to give the rubber sole a bit of extra contact with the rock.

THE SECRET LANGUAGE OF CLIMBING

gritstone sandpapery granite rock that offers lots of grip

friction climbing using holds that rely on friction, rather than a hard edge, for grip

The important thing is to trust the hold once you are sure it works. The more weight you put on your foot, the more grip you will have.

Joshua Tree

The Joshua Tree National Park is one of the world's best-known climbing destinations. Most climbers try to stay at a campsite called Hidden Valley—unfortunately, this is now so popular that it can be hard to get a spot there. But the site is a great place to start exploring the thousands of climbs in the area.

JOSHUA TREE
Location: California
Type of climbing: famous for routes using cracks
Difficulty level: 3 of 5
Best season: all year

One of the many spectacular jamming routes in the Joshua Tree National Park.

WHY JOSHUA TREE?

There is a big variety of climbing here, but one of the things Joshua Tree is most famous for is climbs that follow cracks. Some of these feature **off-widths**—cracks too big for easy hand and foot jams. These are hard work to climb, and most people huff and puff their way to the top. There is a big sense of satisfaction from conquering a tricky off-width, though!

If you like Joshua Tree ...

you could also try:
• Yosemite Valley, California
• Mount Buffalo and Big Hill, Australia
All have some great jamming routes.

Jamming

There are lots of different ways of using vertical cracks in the rock face as holds for hands or feet. They are all based around jamming different parts of your body into the crack, so these techniques are called jams. Here are just a few jams:

This short jamming route required a bit of everything—hand jams, fist jams, and foot jams—because there were no other holds.

CLIMBING IN JOSHUA TREE

Beginners and intermediate climbers: Lost Horse is a good place for beginners to head for. There are hundreds of climbs here, including **face climbs** and a LOT of cracks.

Experts: Head for Real Hidden Valley, an old hideout for cattle thieves, which has some very tough routes.

Other tips: In winter, Indian Cove is often the warmest, most sheltered climbing area.

• **Hand jam 1:** Push your fingers into the crack; then twist your hand down until it is jammed.

• **Hand jam 2:** Push your hand into the crack, then push your knuckles against the rock. This one carries a high risk of skin removal!

• **Fist jam:** Put your hand straight into the crack and then make a fist.

• **Forearm jam:** Jam your forearm into the crack and push against the sides.

It's hard (in fact, it's just about impossible) to look elegant using these techniques. But they do work!

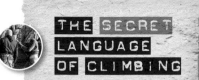

THE SECRET LANGUAGE OF CLIMBING

off-width wide vertical crack in a rock face

face climb climb up an open rock face

The High Tatras

The High Tatras Mountains are on the border between Slovakia and Poland. These ancient peaks are the tallest mountains in this part of Europe. With steep, forested valleys and deep lakes, this is a beautiful place to climb.

THE HIGH TATRAS
Location: Tatras Mountains, Slovakia
Type of climbing: sport climbing
Difficulty level: 3 of 5
Best season: July to September

To be allowed to climb harder routes such as this one in the Tatras, you must be a member of a climbing club.

Tip from a local

Leave a note with your campsite saying when you expect to be back from a climb—they send out a rescue team if you are more than six hours late.

WHY THE HIGH TATRAS?

The Tatras are a great place for those who like to enjoy nature without crowds. This is one of the few places in Europe where you can climb great routes all day without seeing other climbers.

Anyone interested in vampires will be keen to hear that the mountains are part of the Carpathian chain—where the legend of Dracula was born. Better string some anti-vampire garlic outside your tent!

Climbing in the High Tatras

Beginners: On beginner routes in the High Tatras, climbers have to go out with a qualified guide, who will show them the best routes.

Intermediate climbers and experts: Most experienced climbers will probably head for Lomnický štít, the second-highest peak in the Tatras. On the west face there are over 30 routes, including the famous Hokejka, which means Hockey Stick. As one of the local guides says: "Every climber in central Europe has dreamed of climbing Hokejka."

If you like the High Tatras ...
you could also try:
- Ekne, Norway
- Valle Encantado, Argentina

Both are crowd-free locations.

THE SECRET LANGUAGE OF CLIMBING

second climber who follows the leader up a route

bolt metal anchor point securely fixed to a rock face

TECHNIQUE
Sport Climbing

Sport climbing is the name for when two climbers do a route together, one after the other. The first climber is the leader. He or she is followed by a **second**.

The leader sets off up the climb. The second acts as belayer.

As the leader reaches a **bolt**, he or she attaches the rope to it using a carabiner and sling. If the leader falls, the bolt will stop him or her from falling all the way to the ground.

Once the leader reaches the top, he or she secures himself to the rock, then calls to the second.

The second starts climbing, removing the carabiners and slings along the way. The leader now acts as belayer, keeping the second from falling.

Clipping a quickdraw (two carabiners linked by a short sling) to a bolt on the rock.

21

Climbing World Cup: On-Sight

On-sight climbing contests don't offer the fast thrills of speed climbing competitions, which are over in a few seconds. Instead, they are drawn out for several minutes, as the climber tries to find his or her way to the top of the wall. Watching is so absorbing that a whole afternoon quickly goes by without you noticing.

Japanese climber Sachi Anma at the World Cup finals in 2007.

SETTING A ROUTE

Each on-sight contest follows a different route. Top climbers design the routes, which always feature a variety of maneuvers. Some sections rely on strength and power; others require excellent balance and technique. Every competitor finds some sections easy and others hard. Only the climbers with good all-round skills have a chance of making it to the top.

CLIMBING ON-SIGHT

The climbers lead the climb—a rope trails behind them, and they have to clip it to the bolts. Saving strength by not stopping to clip on to every bolt is not allowed. Most climbers take a rest when they reach a big, comfortable hold: they change hands and **shake out** before carrying on.

Angela Eiter of Austria clears a tricky overhanging section during an indoor climbing contest.

Technical: How on-sight climbing contests work

The climbers try to finish the route one after the other. The competitor who reaches the highest hold wins.

The climbers get a few minutes to study the route before the competition starts. They are not allowed to discuss it with each other.

The climbers are taken to an isolation room. Then the first climber comes out and starts to climb. Once a competitor has fallen, he or she is allowed to watch the other climbers.

There are rules for judging who gets highest: touching a hold as you try to reach it is not the same as getting a good grip on it—but it counts as getting higher than only reaching the hold below.

If two or more competitors reach the same point, or the top, the organizers change the holds to make a different route. The climbers go again until one emerges as the winner.

The Gunks

"The Gunks" is the climbers' name for Shawangunk Ridge. Many of the classic routes here were first climbed in the 1930s. Today, The Gunks is still one of the most popular climbing areas in North America, and over 40,000 climbers visit the cliffs each year.

THE GUNKS
Location: New York
Type of climbing: traditional
Difficulty level: 3.5 of 5
Best season: April to November

WHY THE GUNKS?

Simply, this is some of the best traditional climbing in this part of North America. Most of the climbs are packed tightly together in four main areas: The Trapps, Near Trapps, Millbrook and Skytop. The climbing here is mainly on cliffs 130 to 295 feet (40 to 90 meters) high, so the routes are relatively short. This makes it easy to test yourself on a big variety of routes in a single weekend.

This photo captures the essence of climbing in The Gunks: sheer cliffs, beautiful views, and some of the best climbing on America's East Coast.

Traditional climbing

THE SECRET LANGUAGE OF CLIMBING

grade measure of how difficult a climb is

protection temporary anchor points

If you like The Gunks ...

you could also try:
• Tremadog, Wales
• Blue Mountains, Australia
Both have a long history of climbing.

The lead climber sets off on a traditional-style route, carrying plenty of protection clipped to his harness.

CLIMBING IN THE GUNKS

Beginners: Beginners will enjoy the top-roped climbing and bouldering in the Peterskill area.

Intermediate climbers and experts: There are hundreds of great routes for intermediate climbers. Experts will want to try High Exposure—a route that some people claim is the best in the world at its **grade**.

Tip from a Local

After a hard day of climbing, try a sunset canoe trip along the Wallkill River for some gentler exercise.

Traditional climbing is similar to sport climbing (see page 21). The difference is that instead of using bolts, leaders place their own **protection** in the rock while climbing.

The leader sets off, with the second acting as belayer.

As the leader climbs, he or she attaches protection to the rock, then clips the rope on. The leader will not know how solidly the protection is attached until he or she falls on it.

Once the leader reaches the top of the climb, he or she clips on to an anchor point.

The second starts climbing, taking the protection off the rock as he or she goes.

Traditional climbing is far more risky than sport climbing, so only very experienced climbers should lead traditional routes.

Majorca

Sun-starved northern European climbers have been visiting Majorca for years. In winter, the island's combination of great climbing and sunshine is unbeatable. But recently Majorca has become famous for a new kind of climbing—deep-water soloing. This involves climbing alone and without protection on coastal cliff faces above the deep sea. Only try it if you're a good swimmer!

This shows clearly how deep-water soloing is pretty safe—as long as you can swim.

MAJORCA
Location: Mediterranean island belonging to Spain
Type of climbing: soloing
Difficulty level: 4 of 5
Best season: year round, but very hot in July and August

THE SECRET LANGUAGE OF CLIMBING

roof horizontal overhang
pitch climbing distance less than the length of a rope—usually 33 feet (10 meters)

WHY MAJORCA?

Majorca has an amazing variety of climbs. Do you want to climb steep cliffs, cracks, overhangs, or **roofs**? You'll find them all here. Most of the climbs are single **pitch**, so it is possible to do several in a day. There is top-roped, sport and traditional climbing, bouldering and—of course—deep-water soloing.

CLIMBING IN MAJORCA

Beginners: Most rock faces have some beginner routes; a good place to start would be in the Boquer Valley, near the island's northern tip.

Intermediate climbers and experts: It's hard to know where to start, but the limestone rock faces of Sa Gubia would be a good place. There are over 100 climbs here for experienced climbers to try.

Tip from a Local

One of the most beautiful times to visit Majorca is in March, when the island is covered in green grass and brightly colored flowers.

If you like Majorca ...

you could also try:
• Pembrokeshire, Wales
• Swanage, England
• Cote d'Azur, France
Each has some great deep-water solo climbs.

SKILL SESSION
Deep-water soloing

Most climbers consider climbing alone and without protection to be far too dangerous. If you slip and fall, there's nothing to stop you from hitting the ground. But what if, instead, you hit the sea? That's the basic idea behind deep-water soloing:

• The climbs all take place on steep cliffs overlooking the deep sea. If climbers fall, they push off backward and land in the sea.

• The climbers wear minimum equipment: usually just rock shoes, shorts and a top.

• Don't try this—obviously—unless you can swim!

The deep-water soloing on Majorca is among the best in Europe. The best cliffs are in a series of beautiful bays on the island's southeast coast.

Yosemite Valley

YOSEMITE VALLEY
Location: California
Type of climbing: all kinds, but famous for long routes
Difficulty level: 5 of 5
Best season: April to October

If there's one place that every rock climber in the world dreams of going, it's the Yosemite Valley in California. The names of the different climbing areas—Tuolumne Meadows, Half Dome, Cathedral Rock and El Capitan—send shivers down a climber's spine. This is home to some of the best, most famous, and longest climbs in the world.

THE SECRET LANGUAGE OF CLIMBING

portaledge lightweight, foldable bed used for sleeping on a rock face

WHY YOSEMITE?

Yosemite has lots of different types and grades of climb, though there are few for beginners. What brings the world's best climbers here year after year is the long, long routes up the giant granite rock faces. Some of these take days to complete, with the climbers sleeping on **portaledges** and hauling their food and drink up behind them.

If heights make you nervous, don't apply for this job. This climber is just below the Great Roof on El Capitan, in the Yosemite Valley.

Tip from a Local

Get someone to show you what poison oak looks like and then avoid it. It's found all over the Yosemite Valley and, if you touch it, your skin will itch like crazy.

CLIMBING IN YOSEMITE

Intermediate climbers:
There are few routes even for intermediate climbers in Yosemite, but there are some good easier-grade climbs at Leaning Tower and Glacier Point Apron.

Experts: Yosemite's most famous climb, and the one everyone would like to do, is The Nose. It takes most people about five days to climb the 2,890 feet (881 meters) to the top. When they finally make it, most have sore limbs, skinned knuckles, and a big smile.

Climbing big walls

There's more to climbing big walls than just the climbing. Careful planning and teamwork are also required:

• **Planning:** making sure you begin with the right equipment for every stage of the climb. It would be a shame to get close to the top, only to discover something crucial had been left behind at camp.

• **Teamwork:** making sure everyone works together as well as possible. When the lead climber finishes a pitch, he or she then has to haul up the team's supplies. The second then starts climbing. Doing this efficiently means less climbing time is wasted.

Good big-wall climbing teams combine top-level climbing technique, excellent organization, and careful advance planning.

Bedding down for the night on a portaledge, high above the Yosemite Valley

If you like Yosemite …

you could also try:
• The Troll Wall in Norway
• Nameless Tower, Pakistan
These are among the world's tallest, toughest rock faces.

Glossary

anchor point secure place to attach a climbing rope

bolt metal anchor point securely fixed to a rock face

bouldering climbing at a low level, not usually higher than 6.5 feet (2 meters), with just a crash mat for safety gear

chickenhead bulging lump of rock (and also the name of a handhold)

crab short for carabiner, a loop of metal with a lockable gate in it

crash mat thickly padded safety mat

face climb climb up an open rock face

friction climbing using holds that rely on friction, rather than a hard edge, for grip

grade measure of how difficult a climb is

granite hard rock with surface like sandpaper

gritstone sandpapery granite rock that offers lots of grip

harness safety equipment fastening around the waist and thighs

holds places where your hands and/or feet can grip the rock

off-width wide vertical crack in a rock face

overhang section of rock face that slopes outward

pitch climbing distance less than the length of a rope—usually 33 feet (10 meters)

portaledge lightweight, foldable bed used for sleeping on a rock face

protection temporary anchor points

roof horizontal overhang

second climber who follows the leader up a route

shake out shake arms and hands to relax the muscles

sling loop of strong nylon tape or rope

sloper sloping (and not very good) handhold

topping out reaching the top of a climb

Other words climbers use

abseil slide down a rope. In North America this is called rappelling

bail retreat from a climb, having realized it is not possible to finish it

bombproof solid: for example, a bombproof (or bomber) hold would be one you can get a really good grip on

brain bucket helmet

chimney crack so big it will fit your whole body

deck out fall and hit the ground. Also known as cratering

gardening picking dirt and plants out of holds on a route that hasn't been climbed before, or isn't climbed very often

on sight leading a climb you have never seen before

redpoint leading a climb with no falls

screamer fall so long that you have time to scream

spanked defeated by a climb

Finding out More

THE INTERNET

FactHound offers a safe, fun way to find Internet sites related to this book. All of the sites on FactHound have been researched by our staff.

Here's all you do:
Visit www.facthound.com
FactHound will fetch the best sites for you!

BOOKS

Rock Climbing and Abseiling Paul Mason (Macmillan Library, 2008) Introduces the basic skills and techniques of rock climbing and gives advice about equipment.

Know Your Sport: Rock Climbing Yvonne Thorpe (Franklin Watts, 2009) Includes step-by-step photographs explaining key techniques and safety measures.

Xtreme Sports: Rock Climbing Kate Cooper (TickTock Media Ltd, 2007) A handy introduction to the sport that includes some famous stories, plus rock-related activities to try.

Index